On Target English

Comprehension and Writing Skills

Year 5

Hilary Frost

Sarah Lindsay

Heather Painter

Longman

Edinburgh Gate
Harlow, Essex

Contents

A Narrow Squeak

"Do you realise," said Ethel, "that tomorrow is our Silver Wedding Day?"

"So soon?" said Hedley in a surprised voice. "How time flies! Why, it seems but yesterday that we were married."

"Well, it isn't," said Ethel sharply. "You only have to look at me to see that."

Hedley looked at her.

She seems to have put on a great deal of weight, he thought. Not that she isn't still by far the most beautiful mouse in the world, of course, but there's a lot more of her now.

"You have certainly grown," he said tactfully.

"Grown?" snapped Ethel. "And whose fault is that, pray? Anyone would think you didn't know why I'm blown out like a balloon. Goodness knows what sort of father you will make."

"A father?" said Hedley. "You mean …?"

"Any time now," said Ethel. "And I'm starving hungry, Hedley. Fetch us something nice to eat, do. I could just fancy something savoury."

She sighed deeply as her husband hurried away. Was there ever such a mouse, she said to herself. *So* handsome, but so *thick*. Let's hope he doesn't walk straight down the cat's throat. I wouldn't put it past him, and then there won't be any Silver Wedding.

Dick King-Smith

Glossary

Silver Wedding *the twenty-fifth wedding anniversary*

Ethel and Hedley

Comprehension

● To understand what
characters are like

Write the correct answer to each question in your book:

1 When is Ethel and Hedley's Silver Wedding Day?

Ethel and Hedley's Silver Wedding Day is tomorrow.
Ethel and Hedley's Silver Wedding Day was yesterday.

2 How has Ethel changed?

Ethel has grown taller.
Ethel has put on weight. ✓

3 What does Ethel want to eat?

Ethel wants to eat something sweet.
Ethel wants to eat something savoury.

4 What does Hedley think about his wife?

He thinks she is the most beautiful mouse.
He thinks she is the fattest mouse.

5 What does Ethel think about her husband?

Ethel thinks her husband is good-looking but stupid.
Ethel thinks her husband is intelligent and sensible.

6 Why does Ethel think there might not be a Silver
Wedding Day?

She thinks Hedley might get himself killed.
She thinks Hedley might get lost looking for food.

Finding out about the characters

The words used to describe how people say things tell us more
about them and their character. Copy this table in your book
and fill it in.

What is said	Who spoke, and how
Do you realise,	said Ethel
So soon?	Hedl
Well it isn't,	
You have certainly grown,	
Grown?	

Use the table to help you answer these questions:

1 What do you know about the character of Hedley?
2 What do you know about the character of Ethel?

Writing

● To write a reading log

Thinking about books

When Mary started this story she decided to keep a **reading log**. This is what her reading log looked like.

Name of book	A Narrow Squeak
Author	Dick King-Smith
About the characters	Hedley doesn't seem to notice things but he is kind and thinks about Ethel's feelings because he doesn't call her fat he just says she's grown. Ethel seems to be quite quick-tempered because she says things 'sharply' and 'snapped'.
What I liked/ disliked	I like the way she says that she is 'blown out like a balloon' instead of saying she's expecting a baby.
Prediction – what I think is going to happen	I think Hedley might have a few problems in the future trying to get food for Ethel. Ethel doesn't trust him and thinks he might be eaten by a cat so I think he might make some bad mistakes.

Choose a story and read the first two or three pages. Looking at the front and back cover will help you decide if you might enjoy reading it.

Write a reading log like Mary's to record your ideas about the story.

Openings

Choose another book and read the first three pages.

Write a paragraph to explain whether you think it has a good opening.

Start like this:

I liked/disliked the opening to this story because …

Tip

Use quotes from the text to back up your opinions.

Remember

You must give reasons for your opinions using the text to back up your ideas.

Trip to a Victorian School

On Wednesday last week, 9th December, our class went back into history! It was a day we shall remember for ages, especially Rob Jones.

We have been learning about life in Victorian times and Mr Dickens arranged for us to visit the Victorian School Museum. We had to go dressed as children did when they went to school over 100 years ago.

As soon as we walked into the school the teachers, who were all dressed in Victorian costumes, started shouting and made us stand in very straight lines. We weren't allowed to look around and Mr Maldoon, the Victorian School Headmaster, pretended he was going to beat us with his cane if anyone even whispered. It was really quite scary!

Next, we were told to sit in a classroom. The desks were in straight lines, and we had slates and chalk for writing. Rob Jones was talking to me, and Mr Maldoon saw him. He shouted and made Rob stand on a chair in front of the class. Rob was wearing his dad's long, stripy trousers, and we all laughed. That made Mr Maldoon really mad.

Now I know how Victorian children must have felt! It was a very interesting day, but I'm pleased I go to school now and not then.

Comprehension

● To put events in order

Helpful words

easier   nervous
pretending   variety
punished   bored

Tip

Questions 4 and 5 need longer answers as you should give your opinions, with your reasons.

About our day

Write these sentences, putting them in the order that they happened:

We sat in a Victorian classroom.

The teachers told us to stand in straight lines.

Mr Maldoon got really cross when we all laughed at Rob.

Rob Jones had to stand on a chair at the front of the class because he was talking.

On Wednesday we dressed in Victorian costumes.

Back in time

Write a sentence or sentences to answer these questions.

1 What does the writer mean by 'went back into history'.

2 Why would Rob Jones particularly remember the visit?

3 Write two things that were different in Victorian schools from schools today.

4 Why do you think the writer prefers going to school now?

5 How do you think Victorian children felt about going to school?

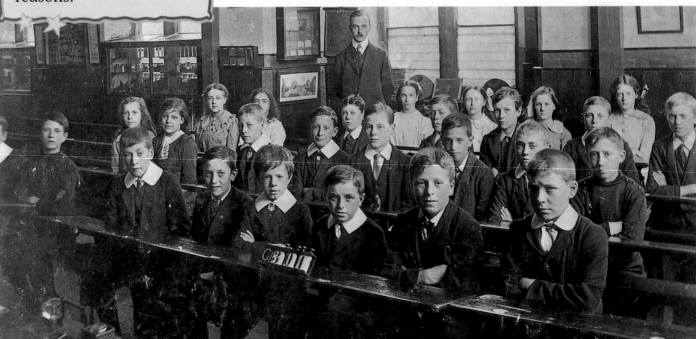

A special trip

Think about a time when you went on a trip with your family or your school.

Copy this table to record your ideas and memories.

Place visited	
Who went	
Date of visit	
Weather conditions	
How we travelled	
What we did	
Time we arrived home	

Writing an account

Use the information in your table to help you to write an interesting account of your trip.

Here are some ideas for how you might organise the paragraphs in your account.

> I went on a visit to _____ on (date)
> _____ .
> I went with _____ .
> To begin with _____ .
> Next _____ .
> Finally _____ .
> Before I went on the visit I thought _____ .
> When I got there I found out _____ .

Remember

Don't forget to include anything unusual or funny that happened.

Your account should have a title.

Stig of the Dump

While on holiday, Barney has made friends with Stig, a strange character who lives in a cave at the bottom of a chalk-pit. They form a good friendship but they don't always agree.

Barney's heart missed a beat. He got slowly to his feet, gripping his spear.

"Fox!" he hissed. "That's it, Stig. It really is a fox." He levelled his hunting spear at the fox, and wished he had the bows and arrows. But perhaps he could spear it.

"Stig!" he breathed. "Come on, now's your chance."

But this time Stig did not raise his bow. Instead, he took hold of the end of Barney's spear and held it so that he could not throw it. The fox strolled calmly up to their very feet, gave Stig a glance, and vanished down the hole.

Barney nearly burst into tears of rage. "But Stig, why did you let him go?" he stormed. "You're *supposed* to kill foxes. That's what hunting's *for*! That's why we *came*!"

But Stig grinned in a rather superior way.

Then, a few moments later, a hound comes looking for the fox …

It came straight for where they were hiding, looked up and saw Stig, and bared its teeth and growled.

Stig bared *his* teeth and growled.

The hound looked surprised. It wasn't sure whether Stig was animal or human, but he was certainly lying between it and a good strong scent.

The hound took a step forward, making horrible noises in his throat.

Stig took a step forward on his hands and knees, making horrible noises in *his* throat.

Barney sat at the back of the little cave, holding his middle. The hound looked very big and fierce and he was afraid it might hurt Stig. But then Stig was looking very fierce too, and he might hurt the hound.

Stig was the first to move. With a lightning spring he darted forward and bit the hound hard on the ear. It was too much for the poor animal. It was not afraid of sharp-toothed foxes or other animals that fought back, but Stig smelt like a man and it had never heard of a man biting a dog. It turned and made off yelping, with its tail between its legs.

Clive King

Stig and Barney go hunting

Write this passage, filling in the gaps so that it makes sense.

When he saw the _____ Barney wanted to kill it with his _____. Stig did not want to kill it so he _____ the spear so that Barney could not throw it. The fox gave Stig a _____ and _____ down the hole. Barney was _____ because he thought that they had come hunting in order to kill _____.

The hound came straight towards their hiding place and bared its teeth and _____. Stig bared his teeth and growled. Both the _____ and _____ looked very fierce. Stig was the first to move, and with a lightning spring, darted forward and _____ the hound on the _____.

The hound went away with its tail _____ its _____.

Comprehension

● To think carefully about a story

Helpful words

hound held foxes growled bit Stig spear vanished fox glance disappeared furious legs ear between cross

An unexpected outcome

Write a sentence to answer each of these questions:

1 Why do you think Stig didn't want to kill the fox?

2 Why do you think 'Stig grinned in a rather superior way'?

3 What was it about Stig that surprised the hound?

4 When Stig was facing the hound how do you think Barney was feeling?

5 Why did the hound run away?

6 Do you think foxes should be hunted? Give your reasons.

Helpful words

hunting growled behave afraid alarmed strange unexpected

Writing

- To think about the pace of a story and to retell it from a different point of view

Remember

Give your story a title.

Highs and lows

1 Write the words and phrases the author has used in the first section of the story to build up the excitement. The first one is done for you:

Barney's heart missed a beat.

2 Write the sentence in the first section of the story that slows the action down.

3 Why has the author put some words in italics?

4 Copy the sentence that you think is the most dramatic part of the whole story.

The hound's story

Retell the story from the point of view of the hound. Start when the hound watches the fox go up to Stig and Barney. If you wish you could start your story like this:

I was exhausted and muddy. I'd chased that fox for miles, or so it felt. I had it cornered, when suddenly it stopped. I watched from behind a tree. I couldn't believe it! After all my efforts, two humans were going to get it!

Designing a Paddle Boat

In this class the children have been studying boats.

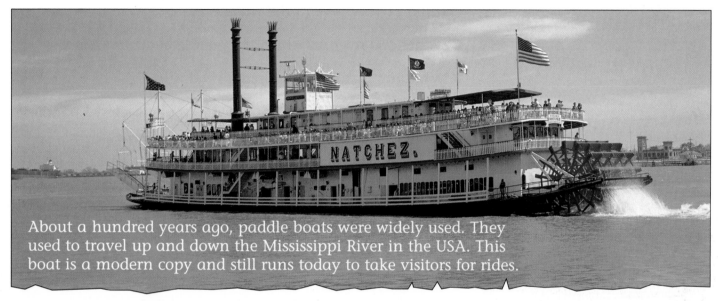

About a hundred years ago, paddle boats were widely used. They used to travel up and down the Mississippi River in the USA. This boat is a modern copy and still runs today to take visitors for rides.

Here are the instructions the children have found for building a model paddle boat.

You will need

- some thick pieces of balsa wood
- some thin pieces of balsa wood
- nails
- a hacksaw

- elastic bands
- small boxes, containers and cartons
- balsa wood glue
- paints

Keep your design simple.

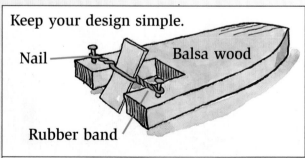

Nail — Balsa wood

Rubber band

Try out models with different widths and lengths. Try it with different size paddles.

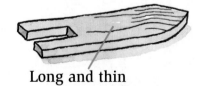

Long and thin

Short and wide

When you think you have the best shape for a paddle boat, use the cartons and boxes to make the upper decks.

Comprehension

- To understand the importance of clear instructions

Helpful words

boxes balsa glue
visitors thick
Mississippi nails
paddle thin cartons

Paddle boats

Write a sentence to answer each of these questions:

1 Explain differences between the ways a paddle boat and a sailing boat move in the water.

2 Name one river on which the paddle boats travelled.

3 What are paddle boats used for today?

4 What type of wood do you need to make a model paddle boat?

5 What should the children use to fix their model together?

6 What will they need to make the upper decks?

Instructions

Look carefully at the diagrams and the list of things you will need on page 13.

Now write instructions for making a paddle boat.

- Write short, simple sentences.
- Take care to write the stages in the correct order.
- Number the sentences in order.
- Draw simple diagrams, if this helps to make things clearer.

The lost game

Writing

● To write clear instructions for a game

A board game has been found but no one knows how to play it. Some hazard cards have been found but more are needed.

Complete the list to say what should be written on the new cards. There should be six cards.

Hazards

1 The paddle boat hits a sandbank – miss a turn.

2

Instructions for the game

Decide how you think the Paddle Boat game might be played.

1 Make a contents list for the games box. Include everything you will need to play this game.

2 Write a list of instructions of how to play this game. Make them very clear for others to follow easily.

Use these headings to set out your work clearly:

The Paddle Boat Game

Contents

●

Instructions

1

Remember

Numbering your instructions shows the order that things have to be done in.

15

The Wind in the Willows

The Mole was quiet for a minute or two. But he began to feel more and more jealous of Rat, sculling so strongly and so easily along, and his pride began to whisper that he could do it every bit as well. He jumped up and seized the sculls, so suddenly, that the Rat, who was gazing out over the water and saying more poetry-things to himself, was taken by surprise and fell backwards off his seat with his legs in the air for the second time, while the triumphant Mole took his place and grabbed the sculls with entire confidence.

"Stop it, *you* silly ass!" cried the Rat, from the bottom of the boat. "You can't do it! You'll have us over!"

The Mole flung his sculls back with a flourish, and made a great dig at the water. He missed the surface altogether, his legs flew up above his head, and he found himself lying on the top of the prostrate Rat. Greatly alarmed, he made a grab at the side of the boat, and the next moment—Sploosh!

Glossary

prostrate *lying out flat with one's face downwards*

Over went the boat, and he found himself struggling in the river. O my, how cold the water was, and O, how *very* wet it felt. How it sang in his ears as he went down, down, down! How bright and welcome the sun looked as he rose to the surface coughing and spluttering! How black was his despair when he felt himself sinking again! Then a firm paw gripped him by the back of his neck. It was the Rat, and he was evidently laughing—the Mole could *feel* him laughing, right down his arm and through his paw, and so into his—the Mole's—neck.

Kenneth Grahame

Comprehension

● To understand how characters are developed in a text

Similar meanings

Find a word in the text that has a similar meaning to each of these words:

1 silent   2 envious   3 rowing   4 grabbed

5 peering   6 complete   7 oars   8 flattened

Helpful words

sculling • jealous • entire • quiet • seized gazing • prostrate sculls •

Rat and Mole

1 The phrases in the box are about Mole and Rat. Sort them into the right columns. Add two more of your own.

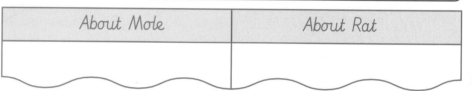

was jealous of his friend, wanted to show off, saw the funny side of things, liked poetry, thought he would be good at rowing, was good at rowing

About Mole	About Rat

Tip

If you don't understand what a word means, look it up in the dictionary.

2 Write only the statements that are true:

Rat and Mole were friends.

Mole could be impetuous.

Rat was unkind to Mole.

Rat looked after Mole.

Rat was used to being on the river.

3 What does the author mean when he writes about Mole …
a 'his pride began to whisper'?
b 'he found himself lying on the top of the prostrate Rat'?

Rat and Mole make a bridge

Mole has asked Rat to help him build a bridge. Prepare a plan for a story which shows how the two characters work together to solve the problems.

Writing

● To write a new scene using the same characters

Helpful words

struggled   idea
collapsed   squashed
soaked

Copy this table to help to organise your notes as you plan your story. Use the pictures to give you some ideas.

Title	Rat and Mole Make a Bridge
Setting	
Characters	
Plot	

Remember

When writing about the plot, make sure you answer these questions:

● What are they going to do and why?
● What is the main event (and what goes wrong)?
● How is it sorted out in the end?

Writing your story

Write the story you have planned.

Think about these points before you start writing.

● You need a really good opening.
  You could start with a description of the setting.
  You could start with a conversation between Rat and Mole.

● Make sure the reader knows how both Rat and Mole are feeling as the story develops.

Tip

Don't make too many things happen or it will get confusing.

19

An Unexpected Surprise

This is part of a play script:

Characters

Jess
William (Jess's brother)
Tom (a friend of Jess and William)
Jake (a robber)
Florrie (Jake's sister and partner in crime)
Policeman

....

The setting is an empty kitchen in an old house. On the table are the remains of a meal: a half-eaten loaf, an empty carton of milk and a piece of cheese. Through a window in the hall lightning can be seen and thunder can be heard.

JESS   Phew! We've made it! I'm not too wet.

WILLIAM   Well I trod in a puddle and my sock is soaking.

TOM   Never mind, at least we've found somewhere dry to shelter until the storm passes.

JESS   *(Jess moves over to the table)* Look over here. I thought this house was empty, the new family are not due to move in until next week.

TOM   *(puzzled)* But someone's been here, and quite recently, because there's bread on the table and it's quite fresh.

(The sound of a thump is heard.)

WILLIAM   What was that? I think there's someone else here. What shall we do?

JESS   Shhh! I can hear voices but I can't hear what they are saying.

WILLIAM   *(whispering)* I think we ought to get out of here. I'm frightened.

TOM   No, let's see if we can see who it is. They might be sheltering from the rain too.

WILLIAM   *(quickly)* Or they might be up to no good.

Taking shelter

Write a sentence to answer each of these questions:

1 How did William get his sock wet?

2 What is the weather like at the start of this play?

3 Why did the children think the house would be empty?

4 Why was Tom puzzled?

5 How do you think the children felt when they first went into the house?

6 Who wanted to run away? Why?

7 Do you think it is a good idea for them to investigate the voices? Explain why you think this.

Become a stage designer

The set, or scenery, is built on stage before the performance takes place.

Imagine you have been asked to design the set for this play.

Draw a plan, looking down on the stage from above. Then draw a picture of how it will look from where the audience will sit.

- Read the play script carefully so that the correct details are included.

- Remember to create places where the actors can come on stage and leave the stage.

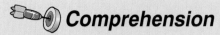 **Comprehension**

- To understand how a play script is written

Helpful words

stepped puddle family remains relieved storm scared nervous adventure exciting unpleasant angry frightened

 Tip

Most of the information you need can be found in the setting at the beginning of the play.

Writing

● To write a play script

What happens next?

Remember

You must tell the story by indicating what the characters say and do.

Write a paragraph to say what you think might happen next in this story.

Use the pictures in this unit and the list of characters to give you ideas.

Writing a script

Now continue the play script using the story ideas that you have written.

Set your work out like this:

Use brackets if you are giving a stage direction or indicating how a line should be said.

WILLIAM	(whispering) I think we ought to get out of here. I'm frightened.
TOM	No, let's see if we can see who it is. They might be sheltering from the rain too.
WILLIAM	(quickly) Or they might be up to no good.

Picture Poems

(to be read from the bottom)

FOXGLOVE

foxglove
push and shove
nearly there
spiral stair
stamen case
freckle-face
blind tunnel
bee funnel
purply-locks
pollen box
tickly sap
pixie cap
scalloped shell
finger bell

SUE COWLING

HOW TO DIVE

Now you're at the highest ever,

Somewhat more assured —

Now you're older,

Second stop,

To begin,

jumpin
belly flop
getting bolder
second highest board
try a dive that's really clever

NOEL PETTY

DEVELOPMENT

THE PRIM
HOUSES PROPER
A
NICE
NEAT
ALSO CLEAN STIFF
CLIPPED
PRIM
NICE PROPER STARCHED
STIFF
STARCHED
NEAT STREET

SHHHHHHHHHHHHH
WHAT HAPPENS
WHEN SOMEONE
WHO LIVES HERE
MAKES A MESS?
HHHHHHHHHHHHH

ROBERT FROMAN

23

Comprehension

To understand how concrete poetry can be set out

Comparing poems

Draw this table and fill in the missing sections.

Title	Foxglove	Development	
Poet			Noel Petty
What word pictures have been made?	The words have been written on the parts of a foxglove.		
Where do you start to read the poem?			At the bottom of the page.
How do you read the words?		Down the street from the top and then down either side of the road.	
Does the poem rhyme?	The words in the pairs of flowers rhyme with each other.		
Is there a pattern in the lines of poetry?			Each line gets longer.

Pictures and poetry

Write a sentence to answer each of these questions:

1 How does the way *How to Dive* is set out tell us what the poem is about?

2 Why has the poet of *How to Dive* started his poem at the bottom?

3 In the poem *Development*, how do the capital letters help to give the message of the poem?

4 Name three things that the poet has said the foxglove is like.

5 Which poem do you like best? Explain the reasons for your decision.

Helpful words

diving board
shape words are part of the picture
size and shape
eye-catching
swimming pool

How to High Jump

Write your own concrete poem.
Use this title: *How to High Jump*

Remember

A concrete poem is one where the words make part of the picture, and the layout is part of the poem.

1 First, collect words and phrases that describe the run up:

feet pounding, ...

2 Now write some ideas about the jumper leaving the ground and going over the high-jump bar:

soaring upwards, ...

3 Finally, write about how the athlete is going to land:

scrunched-up landing mat, ...

Fun with poetry

Experiment with ideas on scrap paper before you decide on the words you are going to use and how you are going to arrange them.

Have fun creating your own concrete poem but think about the following as you write:

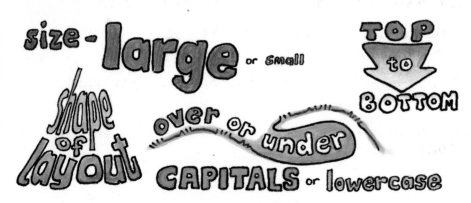

25

Flying Machines

Here are some pages from some CD-ROM encyclopedias.

HIGH AND LOW, FAST AND SLOW

Concorde

Hot-air balloon

Glider

Many different kinds of machines can fly. Supersonic airplanes like Concorde have very powerful engines. They can fly faster than the speed of sound and at heights three times higher than the highest mountain.

Gliders and hot-air balloons, on the other hand, rely on air currents to move them around very slowly and gently.

The design of each aircraft is different, depending on the job it needs to do.

HELICOPTERS

Helicopter

Each arm of the rotor blade on a helicopter is a small wing. The pilot adjusts the angle of the rotor blade to make the helicopter climb straight up, move forward or fly backwards, or just hover.

Helicopters are very useful aircraft for flying in and out of areas that don't have runways.

SPACE SHUTTLES

Space shuttle

Space shuttles are fired high into space by powerful rockets. They deliver objects into orbit around the Earth.

When a space shuttle returns to Earth, it is travelling faster than any other aircraft has ever flown. This means it gets extremely hot, so it has a very special 'skin' to stop it burning up.

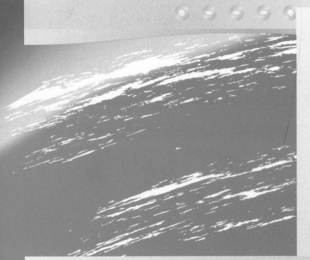
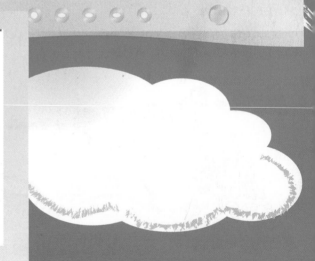

Comprehension

- To find information efficiently and confidently

Finding information

Write the heading of the section in which you can find the information to answer these questions:

1 What type of flying machine is used when there is no runway?

2 Which flying machines rely on air currents to move them around?

3 Which flying machine travels so fast that it gets extremely hot?

4 Which flying machines can travel faster than the speed of sound?

5 Which flying machine can fly backwards?

6 Name two flying machines that fly higher than the highest mountains.

Which and why

Write a sentence to answer these questions:

1 Which flying machine would you use to travel quickly to a meeting in New York? Why?

2 Which flying machine would be best for a quiet trip across the countryside looking at the view? Why?

3 Which flying machine would be used to rescue people from a sinking boat? Why?

4 Which flying machine is used to explore space? Why?

5 Which flying machine would you most like to travel in? Why?

Remember

Look closely at the text to locate where the answer will be found.

Helpful words

space shuttle helicopter
Concorde hot-air balloon
glider peaceful hover
rockets supersonic speed

27

Writing

- To change notes into text for others to read

Using notes

Use these notes to write extra sentences for each page of the CD-ROM encyclopedias.

> Space shuttles – manned – now reusable – invented USA

> Helicopters – first used in Second World War – police observation – passenger services

> Balloons – first voyage Montgolfier brothers 1783 – advertising

> Concorde – French/British co-operation to build – came into service 1976

The first one is done for you:

Space shuttles

The space shuttle was invented in the USA to take people into space. Unlike early space rockets, the shuttle returns to Earth and can be used again, so saving money.

Writing a book

Concorde

Hot-air balloon

Helicopter

Space shuttle

Glider

You are writing an information book about flying machines for a child who is only about six years old.

Think carefully about the words he or she will be able to understand.

You need to write short, clear sentences about each of the flying machines to emphasise their differences.

Put the heading for each page first.

How the Ostrich Got His Long Neck

This folktale has been told through many generations of the Kikayu people in Africa.

Mr Ostrich was a sober-minded, serious husband, who was always willing to assist his wife in her family duties. "My dear," he said to her one evening, when their large clutch of eggs seemed almost ready to hatch, "my black feathers cannot be seen in the darkness, so *I* will guard our eggs by night, and at the same time keep them warm for you. That will leave you free to relax and enjoy yourself until daybreak each morning."

It was a full moon when he came to settle down. The silvery light shed strange shadows and threw up ghostly figures among the surrounding mounds of earth. His head was beginning to nod with weariness, when he became aware of his wife's hissing laugh. He was wide awake in a moment. Straining his short neck to its utmost limit, he saw her dodging around in a game of hide-and-seek with a handsome young ostrich in hot pursuit.

He did not dare leave the precious eggs but every time he heard her foolish giggles he strained and stretched his neck, trying to see what was going on. At last the long, tedious night came to an end. As it did so, his wife appeared out of the grey distance to take over her duties once more.

The ostrich rose stiffly and felt a strangeness in the muscles of his neck. He looked down at his feet, and was alarmed to discover how very far from his head they were – and realised with a shock that, as a result of all the straining, his neck had stretched. He tried to shake it back to its former length, but no matter what he did, it just stayed the same; he had stretched it beyond return.

And that is why the ostrich has a long neck – a lasting memory of a flighty wife.

Adapted from a collection of African Folklore by Phyllis Savory.

29

Comprehension

- To look carefully at a fable

Helpful words

shocked hatching
hissing relax laugh
serious enjoy fun-loving
alarmed warm playful
sober-minded

Right order

These sentences are in the wrong order.
Write them in the correct order so that they tell the story about how the ostrich got his long neck.

Mr Ostrich rose stiffly to his feet and looked down.

Her husband offered to sit on them so that she could enjoy a break.

He was shocked to realise that his neck had stretched and would not return to its former length.

At dawn Mrs Ostrich returned to the nest to take over sitting on the eggs.

Mrs Ostrich was sitting on a clutch of eggs.

All night long she played with a handsome young ostrich while her husband strained his neck to see what was going on.

Mr and Mrs Ostrich

Write a sentence to answer each of these questions:

1 What kind of husband was Mr Ostrich?

2 Why did Mr Ostrich want to sit on the eggs?

3 As Mr Ostrich was falling asleep, what woke him up?

4 Why didn't Mr Ostrich get up and see what his wife was doing?

5 How did Mr Ostrich feel when he first stood up?

6 What kind of wife do you think Mrs Ostrich was?

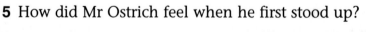
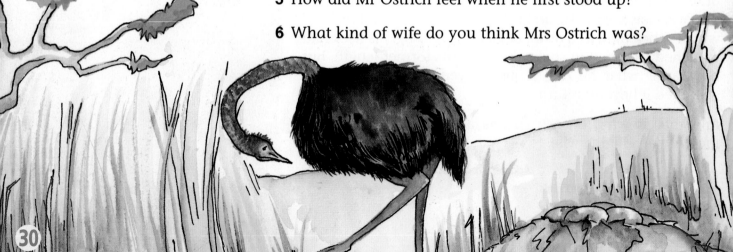

Writing

- To write in the style of a fable

Planning the story

This is how the story plan of *How the Ostrich Got His Long Neck* might have looked.

Title	How the Ostrich Got His Long Neck
Characters	Mr Ostrich – sober-minded, serious Mrs Ostrich – flighty, fun-loving 
Setting	By an ostrich nest full of eggs, among some mounds of earth.
Plot	Mr Ostrich sat on the nest overnight to give his wife a break but he spent all night straining to see what she was doing. She was running around with a young, male ostrich.
Resolution	In the morning Mr Ostrich's neck had stretched so much that it would not return to its former size.

Make a table like this for a story of your own.
Choose one of these titles:

How the Cat Got Its Long Tail
Why the Frog Jumps so High
How the Thrush Found His Song
How the Ladybird Got Its Spots

Story writing

Use your plan to write your story.
Choose the words that you use carefully so that the reader can imagine your story clearly.

Remember

Organise your writing into paragraphs.

Tip

When you have finished writing check your work to make sure you have put capital letters and full stops in the right places.

How Sound Works

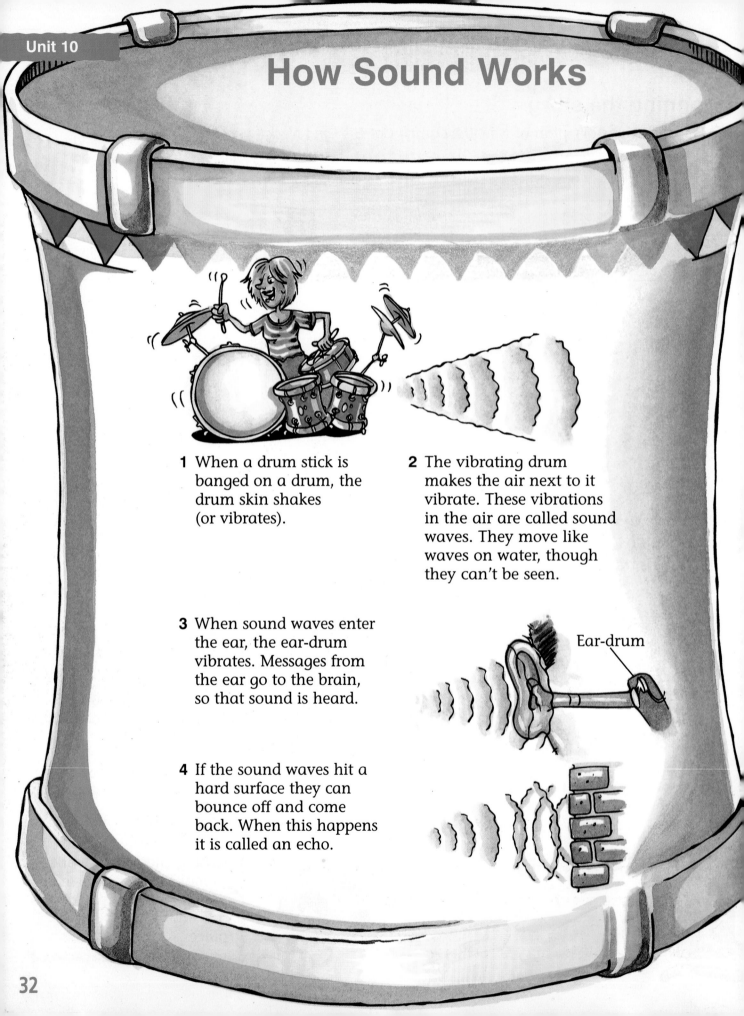

1 When a drum stick is banged on a drum, the drum skin shakes (or vibrates).

2 The vibrating drum makes the air next to it vibrate. These vibrations in the air are called sound waves. They move like waves on water, though they can't be seen.

3 When sound waves enter the ear, the ear-drum vibrates. Messages from the ear go to the brain, so that sound is heard.

Ear-drum

4 If the sound waves hit a hard surface they can bounce off and come back. When this happens it is called an echo.

True or false

Write these sentences in your book.
Write *true* or *false* beside each sentence.

1 Sound waves are vibrations in the air.

2 If sound waves hit a hard surface they disappear.

3 Our ear-drums vibrate when sound waves enter the ear.

4 Sound waves in the air can be seen.

5 The brain receives messages from the ear when the ear-drum vibrates.

6 Vibrations occur when a drum stick is banged on a drum.

Explanations

Comprehension

● To understand explanations

Write some sentences to explain the following:

1 What would happen to the sound if you banged a triangle?

2 How does your ear hear the music of a guitar?

3 Explain what has happened when you call a name in a cave and you hear it more than once.

Helpful words

vibrations sound waves
travel ear-drum pluck
strings messages brain
surface echo

33

Writing

- To write a clear report

Noise pollution

A shopkeeper has made a complaint about the noise pollution in his street.

You have been sent to Manor Street on Saturday 3rd May at 2.00 p.m. to look into the complaint.

You will need to make notes on the noise pollution before writing a detailed report.

List all the sources of noise pollution in the Noise Report on page 35. Indicate the worst ones with a star (✱).

Hide and Seek

Call out. Call loud: "I'm ready! Come and find me!"
The sacks in the toolshed smell like the seaside.
They'll never find you in this salty dark,
But be careful that your feet aren't sticking out.
Wiser not to risk another shout.
The floor is cold. They'll probably be searching
The bushes near the swing. Whatever happens
You mustn't sneeze when they come prowling in.
And here they are, whispering at the door;
You've never heard them sound so hushed before.
Don't breathe. Don't move. Stay dumb. Hide in your blindness.
They're moving closer, someone stumbles, mutters;
Their words and laughter scuffle, and they're gone.
But don't come out just yet; they'll try the lane
And then the greenhouse and back here again.
They must be thinking that you're very clever,
Getting more puzzled as they search all over.
It seems a long time since they went away.
Your legs are stiff, the cold bites through your coat;
The dark damp smell of sand moves in your throat.
It's time to let them know that you're the winner.
Push off the sacks. Uncurl and stretch. That's better!
Out of the shed and call to them: "I've won!
Here I am! Come and own up I've caught you!"
The darkening garden watches. Nothing stirs.
The bushes hold their breath; the sun is gone.
Yes, here you are. But where are they who sought you?

Vernon Scannell

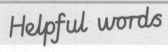

Comprehension

- To understand a narrative poem

Helpful words

excited clever sunset
winter lonely afternoon
seaside breathe
unimportant blindness
searching greenhouse

The story in the poem

Write these sentences in the right order so that they say what happened in the poem:

The children who were searching have all gone away.

The child pushes off the sacks and comes out of the shed to find the others.

The child has found a good hiding place in the toolshed.

The child begins to get cramped and cold.

The child stays very still when the other children come to search near the shed.

The child shouts, "I've won!"

Finding out more

1 Name what the child smells in the toolshed.

2 At what time of day do you think this poem takes place? Give reasons for your answer.

3 At what time of year do you think this poem takes place? Give reasons for your answer.

4 How do you think the child felt when the others came near to the toolshed?

5 What words has the poet used to show that the child stayed very still?

6 What does the child think the others have done after they have left the toolshed?

7 How do you think the child felt on leaving the shed at the end?

A different point of view

This poem tells the story of a game of hide and seek from the point of view of the child who was hiding.

Poets often use the senses to make us imagine the scene more easily.

Touch	'the cold bites through your coat'
Taste	'sand moves in your throat'
Sight	'The darkening garden watches. Nothing stirs.'
Smell	'The sacks in the toolshed smell like the seaside.'
Hearing	'someone stumbles, mutters; Their words and laughter scuffle'

Write the story from the point of view of one of the searchers.
Say what the person did and how he or she felt.
Use descriptions of the different senses to make your account really vivid.

Writing

- To write a narrative poem

Writing a poem

Write your account as a poem.
Write your poem as if you are the person searching.
You could start your poem like this:

Rushing towards the bushes, searching beneath branches,

Stumbling _____

- Pick out the words and phrases from your writing that help to create the atmosphere.
- Leave out linking phrases like 'and then' and 'next I went' as these slow down the pace of the poem.
- Use a thesaurus to find other descriptive words you might use in your poem.

Tip

Short sentences or phrases help to build up tension.

Helpful words

laughing excitedly
busily checking
chilly wind   cold fingers
wandered guiltily
forgot

Tikkatoo's Journey

This is an Inuit folktale. Tikkatoo's grandfather, Nanook, is ill and he needs a flame of fire from the Sun to help him recover. Tikkatoo is the only one who will go on this journey. On his adventures he is directed by the Iceberg to visit Sedna, goddess of the sea and the moon and eventually he is taken on a sledge pulled by a dog to visit the Sun.

Brighter and brighter it grew, larger and larger it loomed. Tikkatoo felt a heat he had never dreamt of, hotter than the fires at home. He had to close his eyes against the glowing light which seemed to burn through his closed lids. The spotted dog stopped. At first, Tikkatoo was almost blinded by the brilliance as he opened his eyes. Then he saw a figure. It was very warm, but it filled him with peace. At last he had found the Sun!

Tikkatoo spoke. "My grandfather, Nanook, is very ill, His heart has been frozen by an ice spirit. Would you give me a flame of your fire to melt the evil magic? I have come a long way for my people."

"I have watched your journey," said the Sun. "You have shown great courage to come so far. I will give you the fire you need. Stretch out your hand."

Into his hand the Sun placed a golden box. Before Tikkatoo could thank her, there was a blinding flash of light, and he felt himself falling through the cold, dark night air on the back of a sunbeam, straight to the centre of his village.

"Who is it? What is it?" they all called.

"It is Tikkatoo," cried his mother.

"Have you got the flame from the Sun?" asked the tallest hunter.

But Tikkatoo didn't answer. He ran straight to the igloo.

Bending low, he entered his grandfather's room and opened the golden box. The room filled with wonderful light and heat. Slowly, Nanook revived. His heart warmed to the heat and the ice spirit melted.

"Tikkatoo," said Nanook.

"Grandfather," cried Tikkatoo and threw his arms around him and hugged him very tight. There they sat, the light dancing about them, as the whole village looked on in amazement.

Amanda Loverseed

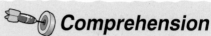

Unit 13

Complete the sentences

Write and complete these sentences:

1 Tikkatoo had to close his eyes against _____

2 When he saw the warm figure of the Sun he felt _____

3 Into Tikkatoo's hand the Sun placed _____

4 Tikkatoo returned to the village on _____

5 When Tikkatoo opened the box the room was _____

6 The whole village looked on in amazement when _____

The Inuit people

Write a sentence to answer each of these questions:

1 What sort of person was Tikkatoo?

2 Why did Tikkatoo undertake this journey?

3 Why did the Inuit people think the Sun was a kind goddess?

4 Why did Tikkatoo have to bend low when he entered his grandfather's home?

5 What lessons might this story be used to teach young Inuit children?

Comprehension

● To practise inferring information from a passage

Tip

Use the text for phrases and words to complete these sentences.

Check carefully to make sure you have spelt the words correctly.

Helpful words

determined   brave
courageous   dependent
entrance   survival
difficulties   igloo

Writing

- To write your own version of part of a folktale

The Iceberg and Sedna, goddess of the sea

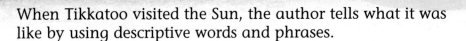

When Tikkatoo visited the Sun, the author tells what it was like by using descriptive words and phrases.

1 Complete this table by writing some descriptive phrases about the Iceberg and Sedna, goddess of the sea.

The Sun	The Iceberg	Sedna, goddess of the sea
hotter than the fires at home	colder than _____ _____	wetter than _____ _____
the heat burned through his closed lids	the cold _____ _____ _____	the wet _____ _____ _____
the warmth filled him with peace	the cold filled him with _____ _____	the wet filled him with _____ _____

2 Write a short description of the Iceberg. Use the picture to help you.

3 Write a short description of Sedna, goddess of the sea. Use the picture to help you.

Tikkatoo's journey under the sea

Write an account of what might have happened to Tikkatoo before he reached the Sun when he met the Iceberg and visited the goddess of the sea.

Use the words, phrases and descriptions you have already written to help you.

Diwali

Pushpa is preparing an article on Diwali. Before she types it up neatly for the school magazine, she has started to edit the first page. Sometimes she chooses more interesting words and sometimes she uses fewer words.

Yesterday we ~~did~~ a play ~~for~~ Diwali.
Yesterday we enjoyed performing a play to celebrate Diwali.

We have ~~done lots~~ of many different ~~sorts of~~ work about light and shadows.
We have been doing many different and interesting activities about light and shadows.

Diwali ~~happens when~~ the Hindu year ~~comes to an end each year.~~
Diwali marks the end of the Hindu year.

~~Lots of~~ people ~~make patterns and things~~ outside the entrances to where ~~they all live which are called~~ Rangoli patterns so we did the same outside our classroom.
People often decorate the entrances to their homes with Rangoli patterns, so we did the same outside our classroom.

The special day of Diwali celebrates the return of Rama to his kingdom.

When Rama came back to his kingdom all the people were very pleased and happy and so they all decided to welcome him back by lighting lots of oil lamps, called divas, to help show him the way home.

The house where they live is cleaned from top to bottom and all the people make sure that their best clothes are clean and ready for this special day.

People dress up in their best clothes and visit their parents, brothers and sisters, uncles and aunts and cousins, to give them cards and presents.

The special day of Diwali is sometimes called the festival of sweets because a special sweet called barfi is eaten on this day. It is a sort of coconut fudge and it is often given as a present to friends and relatives.

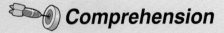

Comprehension

● To compare information

Spot the mistake

Spot the mistake in each sentence, then write it correctly:

1 Pushpa is writing an article for the local newspaper.

2 Pushpa has edited her work to make it longer.

3 She enjoyed performing a dance to celebrate Diwali.

4 She has enjoyed doing many interesting activities about darkness and shade.

5 Diwali is at the beginning of the Hindu year.

6 She has made Rangoli patterns outside her school.

Comparing Christmas and Diwali

Use the text to compare the Christian celebration of Christmas with the Hindu celebration of Diwali. Copy this table and fill in the missing column.

Compare	Christmas	Diwali
The decorations	Tinsel and baubles are used to decorate Christmas trees.	
Reason for the festival	The birth of Jesus	
How light is used	Candles are lit near the nativity scene. Fairy lights on trees	
Gifts	presents and cards	
Special food that is eaten	turkey, Christmas pudding, mince pies	

Helping out

Pushpa has not edited her second page of writing. The first two sentences have been written here again to show you how they could be edited. Look back to page 45 to see how Pushpa first wrote them.

 **Writing**

● To edit a piece of writing

> The special day of Diwali celebrates Rama's return to his kingdom.
>
> When Rama returned everyone was very pleased and excited. They decided to welcome his return by lighting many oil lamps, called divas, to help guide him home.

Tip

Read through your completed work carefully to make sure you have improved it.

Now edit the rest of the text.

Remember:

● words can be taken out ● other words can be put in
● you can change the order of the words

Lakshmi, the goddess of wealth

Edit this writing so that it could be included in Pushpa's article.

Lakshmi who is the goddess of wealth is also worshipped and prayed to at Diwali.

Businesses close all the old accounts of all their customers and open new account books for all their customers on this day because they think she will bring them good luck for the rest of the year if they do this.

In the picture of the goddess Lakshmi you can see it shows her with extra arms. This is supposed to show that the goddess was much more powerful than ordinary people. She is usually shown in pictures standing on a lotus flower with two elephants spraying her from either side.

The people clean their houses so that the goddess Lakshmi will want to visit their home and will then bring them wealth for the whole of the next year.

The Lion and Albert

There's a famous seaside place called Blackpool,
    That's noted for fresh air and fun,
And Mr and Mrs Ramsbottom
    Went there with young Albert, their son.

A grand little lad was young Albert,
    All dressed in his best; quite a swell
With a stick with an 'orse's 'ead 'andle,
    The finest that Woolworth's could sell.

They didn't think much to the Ocean:
    The waves, they were fiddlin' and small,
There was no wrecks and nobody drownded,
    Fact, nothing to laugh at at all.

So, seeking for further amusement,
    They paid and went into the Zoo,
Where they'd Lions and Tigers and Camels,
    And old ale and sandwiches too.

There were one great big Lion called Wallace;
    His nose were all covered with scars –
He lay in a somnolent posture,
    With the side of his face on the bars.

Now Albert had heard about Lions,
    How they was ferocious and wild –
To see Wallace lying so peaceful,
    Well, it didn't seem right to the child.

So straightway the brave little feller,
    Not showing a morsel of fear,
Took his stick with its 'orse's 'ead 'andle
    And pushed it in Wallace's ear.

You could see that the Lion didn't like it,
    For giving a kind of a roll,
He pulled Albert inside the cage with 'im,
    And swallowed the little lad 'ole.

Then Pa, who had seen the occurrence,
    And didn't know what to do next,
Said "Mother! Yon Lion's 'et Albert",
    And Mother said "Well, I am vexed!"

Then Mr and Mrs Ramsbottom –
    Quite rightly, when all's said and done –
Complained to the Animal Keeper,
    That the Lion had eaten their son.

The keeper was quite nice about it;
    He said "What a nasty mishap.
Are you sure that it's *your* boy he's eaten?"
    Pa said "Am I sure? There's his cap!"

The manager had to be sent for.
    He came and he said "What's to do?"
Pa said "Yon Lion's 'et Albert,
    And 'im in his Sunday clothes, too."

Then Mother said, "Right's right, young feller;
    I think it's a shame and a sin,
For a lion to go and eat Albert,
    And after we've paid to come in."

The manager wanted no trouble,
    He took out his purse right away,
Saying "How much to settle the matter?"
    And Pa said "What do you usually pay?"

But Mother had turned a bit awkward
    When she thought where her Albert had gone.
She said "No! someone's got to be summonsed" –
    So that was decided upon.

Then off they went to the P'lice Station,
    In front of the Magistrate chap,
They told 'im what happened to Albert,
    And proved it by showing his cap.

The Magistrate gave his opinion
    That no one was really to blame
And he said that he hoped the Ramsbottoms
    Would have further sons to their name.

At that Mother got proper blazing,
    "And thank you, sir, kindly," said she.
"What waste all our lives raising children
    To feed ruddy Lions? Not me!"

Marriott Edgar (1932)

49

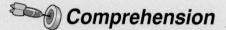

Comprehension

- To give accurate answers about a poem

Helpful words

foolish   naughty
uninteresting   boring
upset   covered   deserved
careless   unsafe   scars

At the zoo

Copy these sentences, choosing the correct ending for each:

1 The Ramsbottoms had gone on a trip to Blackpool because it was famous for _____
- the zoo.
- the shops.
- fresh air and fun.

2 Albert's stick was decorated with a _____
- lion's head.
- horse's head.
- tiger's head.

3 When Albert first saw Wallace the lion was _____
- wild.
- peaceful.
- ferocious.

4 Albert pushed his stick into Wallace's _____
- side.
- eye.
- ear.

5 Mr and Mrs Ramsbottom were sure that Albert had been eaten because all that was left was his _____
- stick.
- cap.
- shoe.

6 The Ramsbottoms were offered money by the _____
- Manager.
- Animal Keeper.
- Magistrate.

What a day!

Write a sentence to answer each of these questions:

1 Why didn't the Ramsbottoms like the sea?

2 What clue is there that Wallace might be ferocious?

3 Why did Albert disturb the lion?

4 Why didn't the Ramsbottoms accept the money from the Manager?

5 The poem says Albert was brave but what do you think about Albert's behaviour?

6 Whose fault do you think it was that Albert was eaten by the lion? Why?

A letter of complaint

Mr and Mrs Ramsbottom are unhappy with their trip to Blackpool and have decided to write a letter of complaint.

Imagine you are the Ramsbottoms and you are writing to the Blackpool Council to complain about your day visit.

Don't forget to say:

- why you were visiting Blackpool
- what happened to you at the zoo
- how you felt about it
- what you want them to do about it

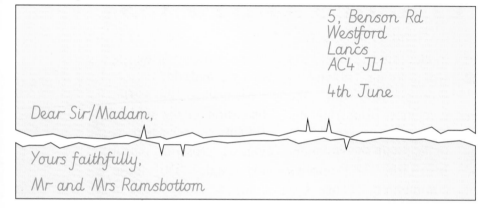

5, Benson Rd
Westford
Lancs
AC4 JL1

4th June

Dear Sir/Madam,

Yours faithfully,
Mr and Mrs Ramsbottom

The reply

Mr Smith has to reply to this letter on behalf of the Blackpool Council.

Imagine you are Mr Smith and compose a letter to Mr and Mrs Ramsbottom.

Don't forget to:

- recommend the town of Blackpool
- sympathise with their problems
- suggest ideas that would prevent any further accidents
- offer compensation

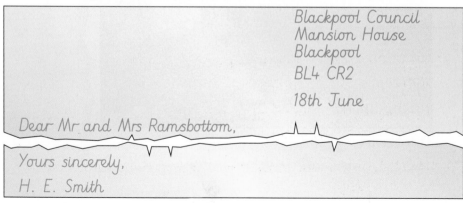

Blackpool Council
Mansion House
Blackpool
BL4 CR2

18th June

Dear Mr and Mrs Ramsbottom,

Yours sincerely,
H. E. Smith

 **Writing**

- To write a letter of complaint

 Remember

Use paragraphs to organise your writing.

Tip

Think carefully about setting out your letter.

51

Clashes at Oldbury

Oldbury News

SERIOUS CLASHES AT BY-PASS

Lorna Drew reports

After years of protest and arguments, yesterday the diggers moved in. Work on the Oldbury by-pass has begun! But if the road builders had thought their problems were over, they were wrong. There were hundreds of people surrounding Mile Lake, the cause of most of the protest. There was also a group of protesters high up in a tree, where they have built a hut. They are almost impossible for the police to reach.

Even though the road builders have paid biologists and botanists from the university to move the rare toads and almost extinct water anemones out of Mile Lake, the protesters don't believe such sites should be destroyed.

Despite the rain and thick mud, protesters were lying down in groups to stop the machines from moving. The police were called in to deal with the situation. Inspector Andrews commented, "This by-pass is seven miles long. It will take hundreds of my officers to prevent the protests, if these people are really determined to interrupt the building work. However, the law is the law, and if that is what is necessary, that is what we shall do."

Meanwhile, the traffic congestion in the middle of Oldbury is as bad as ever. A crossing patrol lady said, "Do those protesters really think a few toads are more important than the safety of our children? The sooner we get these hundreds of heavy lorries out of Oldbury and on to the new by-pass, the better!"

Protesters' huts near Mile Lake

Fact or opinion

Copy these sentences and write *fact* or *opinion* beside each one.

1 *Lots of people surrounded Mile Lake.*

2 *The protesters have built a hut high up in a tree.*

3 *It will be difficult to prevent the protest.*

4 *The protesters think that toads are more important than children.*

5 *The protesters were lying down in the mud and rain.*

6 *The builders thought their problems were over.*

7 *Biologists and botanists have been paid to move the toads and water anemones.*

Different points of view

With an issue like this there are often many different reasons for people's attitudes.

This newspaper article has tried to give some of them.

Write a sentence to explain the views of each of the following people.

Write as if you are each person. Start your work like this:

I think that _____ because _____

1 a protester

2 the police inspector

3 the crossing patrol lady

4 a road builder

5 a lorry driver

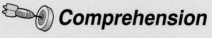

Comprehension

● To tell the difference between fact and opinion

Helpful words

survive   nature
preserve   congested
safer journey
avoid   conflict

Writing

- To write a leaflet presenting an argument

Tip

Bullet points are a good way of drawing people's attention to the most important points.

For and against

Here are some more arguments for and against the building of the Oldbury by-pass.

Sort them into the right columns.

Add two more points to support each argument.

> It will relieve congestion in the town.
>
> It will destroy the habitat of rare toads and special water anemones.
>
> There will be less pollution in the town.
>
> Good farming land will be destroyed.
>
> Children will be safer crossing roads.

For building the by-pass	Against building the by-pass

Design a leaflet

Design a leaflet that could be handed out in town to try to persuade others to think like you.

Choose for yourself which point of view you want to present.

Remember! Your leaflet should:
- make points clearly and quickly
- be easy to read
- use persuasive language
- have impact

Zlata's Diary

Unit 17

Zlata lived in Sarajevo during the Bosnian War. She kept a diary, which she addressed as Mimmy, where she recorded events as they happened. This is part of one of the entries.

Saturday, 2nd May, 1992

Dear Mimmy,

Today was truly, absolutely the worst day ever in Sarajevo. The shooting started around noon. Mummy and I moved into the hall. Daddy was in his office, under our flat, at the time. We told him on the interphone to run quickly to the downstairs lobby where we'd meet him. We brought Cicko [the canary] with us. The gunfire was getting worse, and we couldn't get over the wall to the Bobars, [their neighbours], so we ran down to our own cellar.

The cellar is ugly, dark, smelly. Mummy, who's terrified of mice, had two fears to cope with. The three of us were in the same corner as the other day. We listened to the pounding shells, the shooting, the thundering noise overhead. We even heard planes. At one moment I realised that this awful cellar was the only place that could save our lives. Suddenly, it started to look warm and nice. It was the only way we could defend ourselves against all this terrible shooting. We heard glass shattering in our street. Horrible. I put my fingers in my ears to block out the terrible sounds. I was worried about Cicko. We had left him behind in the lobby. Would he catch cold there? Would something hit him? I was terribly hungry and thirsty. We had left our half-cooked lunch in the kitchen.

When the shooting died down a bit, Daddy ran over to our flat and brought us back some sandwiches. He said he could smell something burning and that the phones weren't working. He brought our TV set down to the cellar. That's when we learned that the main post office (near us) was on fire and that they had kidnapped our President ...

This has been the worst, most awful day in my eleven-year-old life. I hope it will be the only one.

Mummy and Daddy are very edgy. I have to go to bed.

Ciao!

Zlata

55

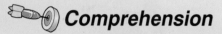

Comprehension

● To understand the feelings of the characters involved

Helpful words

gunfire happened
warning safe sheltering
devastated damaged
shattered worried
occupy comfort
remember

Taking cover!

Write this passage and fill in the missing words and phrases:

Zlata and her mother and father went to shelter in their
_____ . Zlata realised that the cellar, which she
hated, might actually save their _____ . She put
her fingers in her ears to block out the sound of
_____ . She was worried about _____
because they had left him behind in the _____ .
She was also very hungry because _____ . Later,
her father ran to the flat to bring back some _____ .
He also brought back _____ so that they could find
out what was happening. She found out that the
_____ and that the President _____ .

Feelings

Write a sentence to answer each of these questions:

1 Why didn't Zlata and her family go to their neighbour's house?

2 What 'two fears' did her mother have to cope with?

3 Why did Zlata say that the cellar began to look 'warm and nice'?

4 What do you think the street outside would look like after the shelling?

5 What do you think Zlata means when she writes that her parents are 'very edgy'?

6 Why do you think Zlata kept a diary and addressed it as Mimmy?

In the action

The first paragraph of Zlata's diary is about **actions** – what happened during an attack.

1 Write brief sentences to explain what they did.

The second paragraph of Zlata's diary describes **feelings** – what it was like hiding in the cellar.

2 Find five adjectives that have been used to describe what it felt like and write them in your book.

3 Copy into your book the part of the text that most helped you to imagine what it was like.

The third paragraph is about what happened later and the **results** of the attack.

4 Write in your book three things that had happened as a result of the attack.

The last paragraph contains Zlata's comments on the day.

Same situation, different place!

Imagine something similar has happened to you and write a diary entry about what it would be like.

In your writing try to include the answers to these questions:

- Where would you have hidden?
- Who would have been with you?
- What would you have taken with you?
- How do you think you would have felt after a day like this?

Writing

- To comment on and make observations about a text

Tip

You could write your account in **four** paragraphs, using a similar structure to Zlata.

57

The Man Who Planted Trees

A man went walking in a wild desolate place in France. He came across an old shepherd living in the hills and asked for shelter for the night. He wrote about what he found there.

The shepherd who didn't smoke went and fetched a little bag and emptied a pile of acorns on to the table. Then he began to inspect them closely, separating the good from the bad. I smoked my pipe. I offered to help. He said he had to do it himself. And seeing how carefully he worked I didn't insist. That was all the conversation we had. And when he had collected a large enough heap of good acorns he divided them up into groups of ten. As he did so he discarded those that were too small or had a tiny split; he examined them minutely. Once he had sorted out one hundred perfect acorns, he stopped and we went to bed.

The next day the shepherd invited the man to accompany him.

When he reached the place he was aiming for, he began to make holes in the ground with his rod, putting an acorn in each and then covering it up again. He was planting oak trees. I asked him if this land was his. He said it wasn't. Did he know who the owner was? No, he didn't. He thought it must be common land, or perhaps it belonged to people who weren't interested in it. He wasn't interested in who they were. And so, with great care, he planted his hundred acorns.

Jean Giono

Matching endings

Choose the correct ending to these sentences:

1 The shepherd fetched a bag | when he'd sorted one hundred perfect acorns.

2 The shepherd inspected the acorns closely, | but he thought it might be common land.

3 He discarded the acorns that were too small or split | and emptied a pile of acorns on to the table.

4 He stopped and went to bed | separating the good from the bad.

5 To make the holes to plant the acorns | he used a rod.

6 He didn't know who the land belonged to | and sorted them into piles of ten.

Observing the shepherd

Write a sentence to answer these questions:

1 Why didn't the visitor help the shepherd to sort out the acorns?

2 Why do you think there was so little conversation that evening?

3 Why did the shepherd sort out the acorns with such care?

4 How do you think the visitor felt about what he had observed?

5 Why do you think the shepherd planted the acorns?

 **Comprehension**

● To give reasons for the actions of characters

Helpful words

solitary usual perfect
habit survival alone
environment interested
curious nature
concentrating

59

Writing

- To continue a piece of writing in the style of the author

Remember

The account should be very detailed with comments about what he observed and reports about what was said.

Helpful words

different beech nuts
saplings growth alive
creatures birdsong
amazed astonished
incredible

The visitor returns

Ten years later the visitor returned to the home of the shepherd. Imagine you are the visitor and write an account of your evening together ten years later.

Write about:
- why the visitor returned
- what changes he found in the appearance of the shepherd and his home
- what they did throughout the evening

Start your writing like this:

Eventually I arrived at the small dwelling set high in the hills. I knocked ...

A walk in the hills

The next day the shepherd set out again to walk in the hills and again the visitor accompanied him.

Continue your story by writing about what the visitor observed on this second walk with the shepherd.

Write about:
- what the shepherd did on this occasion. Had he changed his habits?
- the changes that the visitor saw
- the effect the changes had on the wildlife
- how the visitor felt about these changes

The Train to Glasgow

Say each verse slightly faster.

Here is the train to Glasgow.

Here is the driver,
Mr MacIver,
Who drove the train to Glasgow.

Here is the guard from Donibristle
Who waved his flag and blew his whistle
To tell the driver,
Mr MacIver,
To start the train to Glasgow.

Here is the boy Donald MacBrain
Who came to the station to catch the train
But saw the guard from Donibristle
Wave his flag and blow his whistle
To tell the driver,
Mr MacIver,
To start the train to Glasgow.

Here is the guard, a kindly man
Who at the last moment pulled into the van
That fortunate boy called Donald MacBrain
Who came to the station to catch the train
But saw the guard from Donibristle
Wave his flag and blow his whistle
To tell the driver,
Mr MacIver,
To start the train to Glasgow.

Wilma Horsebrough

61

Comprehension

- To identify patterns in a poem

Helpful words

whistle   start
Donald MacBrain
flag   Mr MacIver
Donibristle   Glasgow
slowing   waving

 Remember

If you are quoting from the poem you should show this by using quotation marks, e.g. 'Wave his flag and blow his whistle'.

Catching the train

Write a word or a phrase to answer these questions:

1 Where was the train going?

2 At what station was the train setting off from?

3 Who drove the train?

4 What did the guard from Donibristle do?

5 What did Mr MacIver have to do when the guard blew his whistle?

6 Who came to the station to catch the train?

Words and patterns

Write a sentence to answer each question:

1 What words introduce each new verse?

2 Describe the pattern of rhymes.

3 How does the line 'Here is the boy Donald MacBrain' change in the fifth verse?

4 Why was he fortunate?

5 What do you notice about the length of the verses?

6 Why is it suggested that the reader should say each verse slightly faster than the one before?

7 Does the poem have a regular rhythm? Why?

A new verse

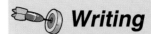

Writing

● To write additional verses to a poem

1 Decide on one character who might be on this train.

2 Think of a phrase to go with your character and write a first line for a new verse like this:

Here is the _____, a cheerful sort

3 Make a list of the words that rhyme with the last word.

4 Now write out the next verse of the poem you have created.

Here is the _____
Who _____
_____ the guard, a kindly man
Who at the last moment pulled into the van
That fortunate boy called Donald MacBrain
Who came to the station to catch the train
But saw the guard from Donibristle
Wave his flag and blow his whistle
To tell the driver,
Mr MacIver,
To start the train to Glasgow.

Helpful words

fort   resort   ought
caught   brought   nought

Travelling companions

1 Decide on four more characters who might be on this train.

2 Write phrases to describe the characters.

3 Choose the best one, and write a new verse for the poem using that character.

Tip

Make sure that the last word in the line has plenty of words to rhyme with it.

Morag and the Monster

Morag MacLeod lives in Scotland and has always wanted to see the Loch Ness Monster.

It was in this path of sunlight that the monster appeared. One moment there was nothing but the blank gold of the ripples dancing, and the next, there was a dark spot among them. The dark spot rose above the water; three more dark patches appeared in line with it among the ripples. From the crowd there came a long sighing sound and somewhere among them a child's voice shrieked, "*The Monster!*"

Morag sat watching it, entranced. It began to move in an easterly direction raising a great flurry of water behind it, its head swaying and the humps behind it rising and falling the way a snake's body does. Then it turned inshore and began to swim in a diagonal line to where Morag was sitting. It came to within thirty yards of her. She could see it clearly – the long neck, the short blunt head, the wide mouth. The sun struck sparkles of light from the greyish humps of its back and she thought, "It must be scales like a fish that's on it, surely, to make it sparkle so."

Then the monster altered course till it was swimming west, parallel with the edge of the loch. Now it looked black against the sun. It dived. Morag scanned the blank surface of the loch. The crowd murmured with disappointment, then they roared as it surfaced again a hundred yards out. The head and one of the humps showed above the surface for a moment, then they disappeared and there was only the dark blue water with the sunlight trail fading from it and the gulls dipping and gliding above it.

Mollie Hunter

Glossary
loch *Scottish word for a lake*

The monster and the loch

This extract describes the appearance of a monster in Loch Ness.
It uses many colourful descriptive phrases.
Sort them into the right columns.

> the blank gold of the ripples dancing
>
> three more dark patches appeared
>
> its head swaying and the humps behind it rising and falling
>
> the sun struck sparkles of light from the greyish humps
>
> the blank surface of the loch

Description of the monster	Description of the loch

Find two more phrases to add to your lists.

Morag's monster

Write a sentence to answer these questions:

1 What made Morag think it looked like a snake?

2 Why did Morag think it looked like a fish?

3 Why did the child in the crowd shriek?

4 How do we know what kind of weather it was?

5 Why did the crowd murmur with disappointment?

6 How do you think Morag felt after seeing the monster?

Comprehension

- To understand how description is used in a text

Helpful words

sunlight scales
frightened excited
disappeared fascinated
apprehensive enchanted
swaying sparkle

 **Writing**

● To write a newspaper article

The interview

Imagine you have been asked to write an article about the monster sighting for the local newspaper.

First you need to interview Morag, a witness to the event.

These are some of the questions you might ask:

The reporter's questions	Morag's replies
1 Where were you when the monster appeared?	I was sitting on a bank with a very clear view of the loch.
2 What did the monster look like?	

Now write two more questions of your own.
Write the replies that Morag might have made.

Writing for the newspaper

Write the article for the newspaper.

Remember to include:
● what happened
● eyewitness accounts
● other opinions about the Loch Ness Monster

Start your article like this:

Early yesterday afternoon, a sighting of the Loch Ness Monster was reported. A large crowd _____

Think of three eye-catching headlines for your writing and choose the best for your article.

Stop the Airport!

We didn't ask for it.

We don't need it! We don't want it!

STOP

THE NEW AIRPORT TERMINAL

More Noise!
More Fumes!
More Congestion!

- **They tell us new aircraft are much quieter.**

If the new aircraft really are quiet, why don't they allow them to land and take off all night?

- **They tell us we'll have more jobs.**

Why do we need more jobs? In this area most people have a job. Take the new airport to a part of the country where people haven't got work.

- **They tell us people need more planes to be able to come to the UK.**

Why not build a brand new airport in another part of the country?

If you don't want your town destroyed,

write to your MP today

A public protest meeting will be held in the Central Hall, Feltenham
on **6th February, at 7.30 p.m.**

Comprehension

- To look at two sides of an argument

To build or not to build

Wildlife under threat

New airport terminal = more visitors to our town = more money being spent

Is bigger better? NO!

Farming land or busy airport?

New airport terminal — jet away on holiday

What arguments could there be for and against the airport being enlarged? Use the picture to help you, but also think of some ideas of your own.

List them under each heading.

For the new airport terminal building	Against the new airport terminal building

Protest, complain, persuade

Answer these questions about the leaflet:

1 What words have been written to gain your attention quickly?

2 What words tell you what to do?

3 If you don't 'write to your MP today', what is being suggested might happen?

4 Do you think this leaflet is presenting a balanced point of view? Explain the reasons for your answer.

Helpful words

advantage   inferred
half truths   influence
opinion   manipulate
facts

68

Save our school

If the new airport terminal is built, Ferndale Primary School will have to close down. The children who are at present attending the school will need to travel three miles to another school. The parents are very cross about this and have arranged to carry protest posters to the town hall to demonstrate their opposition.

Writing

● To learn to write in a persuasive way

1 Make a list of five different points the parents might want to make.

2 Make a list of three points the children might want to make.

3 Use the parents' and children's arguments to write slogans suitable for the protest posters.

Remember

Slogans must express a point of view in just a few words.

Writing to a newspaper

You are a pupil at the school and you have decided to write a letter to a newspaper to explain your point of view and persuade others to support your campaign.

Remember:

● Start your letter by stating your point of view.
● Give at least three reasons for arguing this point of view.
● Show that you understand there is another point of view, but ask people to support you.

Set out the top of your letter like this:

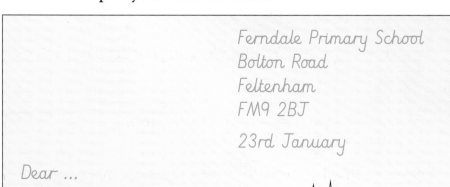

Ferndale Primary School
Bolton Road
Feltenham
FM9 2BJ

23rd January

Dear ...

Almaz

This is part of a story about a young girl called Almaz who lives in Ethiopia. Almaz's mother has died and her father has married a young woman called Kibret. Almaz is worried about how she will get on with her stepmother.

Days later, when all the guests were gone, Almaz's father called her over. "Kibret is your new mother," he said. "Although she is young, you must respect her and do as she says."

Kibret kissed Almaz on both cheeks but did not look up.

Next morning and every morning after, Almaz brought water from the stream. Then her father sent her out to watch the cows and feed the chickens and grind the corn and chop the wood. At night, when the sun stooped over the hills, she came inside.

From the shadows she watched Kibret pour the water for her father's hands and serve the *wat* and *injera*. Then Kibret would sit and eat tiny bites, and after they were finished she would bring the water and food for Almaz.

Once when Kibret was pouring the water for her hands, Almaz said, "May I see the new things you got for your wedding?"

But Kibret looked down and said nothing, so Almaz did not ask again.

Jane Kurtz

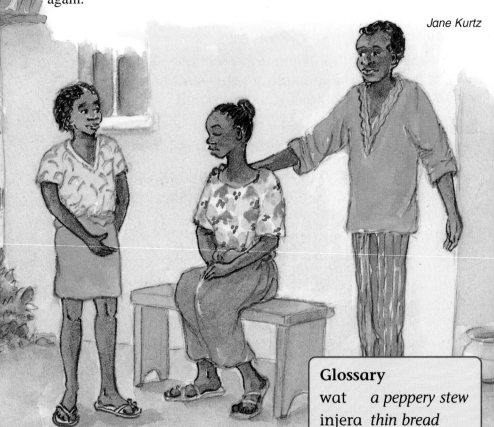

Glossary

wat   *a peppery stew*
injera *thin bread*

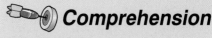

Almaz's day

Choose the correct word to complete these sentences:

1 This story comes from _____

Ethiopia
Nigeria
Britain

2 Almaz's new mother, Kibret, was
_____

young
old
wise

3 During the day Almaz watched the
_____

sheep
cows
chickens

4 Almaz was _____ all day.

lazy
unhappy
busy

5 In the evening Almaz's father ate his
food _____ her.

with
after
before

Almaz and Kibret

1 Why had there been guests in the house?

2 Why do you think Kibret did not look up when she met Almaz?

3 Why do you think Almaz watched Kibret from the shadows?

4 Why do you think Kibret did not show Almaz the new
things she got for her wedding?

5 How do you think Almaz felt when Kibret did not reply to
her request?

6 What are the main differences between Almaz's way of life
and yours?

Comprehension

● To understand why the
characters behave in the
way they do

Helpful words

nervous   wedding
celebration   shy   curious
uncaring   interested
frightened   unkind
embarrassed   lonely
uncomfortable

Writing

- To write from a different point of view

Kibret's day

Use the pictures to help you make a list of four things that Kibret might do in a day and write them in the first column of the table.

In the second column write how you think she might be feeling.

What Kibret might do	How Kibret is feeling about it
1 Get up early to prepare a meal	She is wanting to please her new husband by giving him a good meal to start his day.
2	
3	
4	

The new stepmother

Write about the events in the extract, but write it from the point of view of Kibret.

Start your writing like this:

After the wedding, when all the guests were gone, I was introduced to Almaz. I felt _____

Don't forget to include:

- all the same incidents as in the extract
- what jobs she would have done during the day
- how she felt about what she was doing
- how she felt about Almaz